Wendish Mythology

Wendish Mythology

Divinities and Religious Traditions of the Western Slavs

Stephen E. Flowers

ISBN: 1-885972-13-X

Published by
LODESTAR
P.O. Box 16
Bastrop, Texas 78602

www.seekthemystery.com

Contents

For the Wends of Texas

Acknowledgments

A debt of continuing gratitude goes to Prof. Dr. Edgar Polomé, who has provided me with years of insight into the Indo-European culture, and who kindly provided his comments on a draft of this book. Thanks also go to the volunteers at the library at the Texas Wendish Heritage Museum in Serbin, Texas. All errors found in the book are entirely my own.

Abbreviations

OCS   Old Church Slavonic
Sorb.   Sorbian (Wendish)

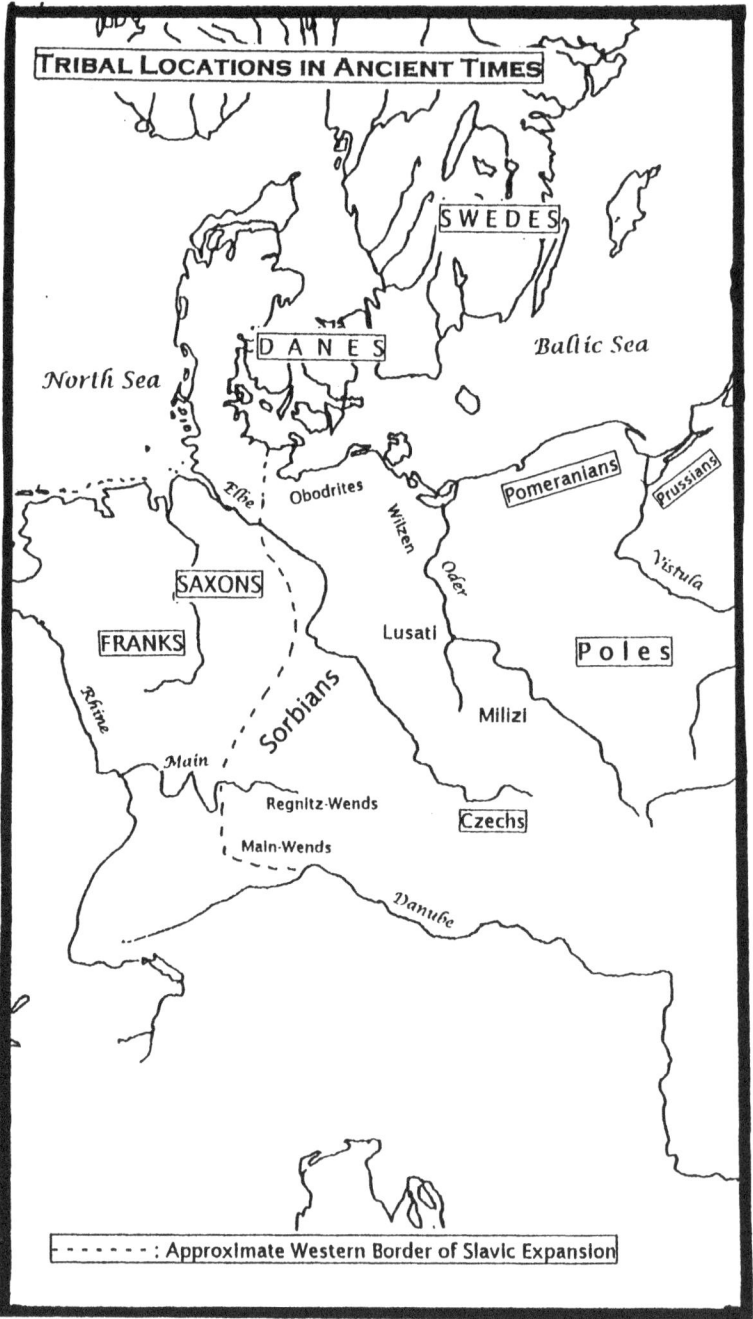

TRIBAL LOCATIONS IN ANCIENT TIMES

SWEDES

DANES

North Sea

Baltic Sea

Pomeranians

Prussians

Obodrites

Elbe

Witzen

Oder

Vistula

SAXONS

FRANKS

Lusati

Poles

Rhine

Sorbians

Milizi

Main

Regnitz-Wends

Main-Wends

Czechs

Danube

- - - - - - : Approximate Western Border of Slavic Expansion

Preface

The Wends of antiquity were a people much feared by their neighbors. They were feared, and sometimes despised, for their tenacious conservation of their traditional ways— which included holding on to their own age-old religious beliefs and their tribal form of government. They were respected by warriors from Sweden to Germany for their courage and cunning in battle. The ancient Wends drew on their own ancestral gods and goddesses for strength and wisdom– for they had a spiritual tradition long before the coming of Christianity. The fact that the Wends — all tribes of the westernmost Slavs — resisted conquest by alien forms of political order and religious rule for as long as they did is largely a testimony to the power of their faith in their ancient divinities and the priesthood which served them. This book is a modest attempt to provide some general ideas of what that old tradition was like.

One of the main reason for writing this little book is personal. In 1993 I moved with my wife from Austin out into the Lost Pines near Smithville, Texas. In this part of the state it doesn't take long before you start to meet folks who will proudly tell you of their Wendish heritage. Much of the reason for this stems from the fine work of the Texas Wendish Heritage Society. As my own academic background lies in the area of ancient mythologies and religions — chiefly focused on the Germanic and Celtic peoples — my curiosity was peaked concerning the ancient Wends: the age-old ancestors of those Wendish pioneers in Texas. My research has resulted in this study, which I especially hope will interest the young people of Wendish heritage. When it is discovered that Wendish history is steeped in heroic warriors, magicians and kings — inspired by mysterious gods and goddesses — a younger generation may find itself more enchanted than it might otherwise have been.

This study necessarily has its limitations. Although the Slavic cultural territory is vast — reaching from the Baltic in the north to the Adriatic and Black Seas in the south and from the Ural Mountains in the east to the Danube river in the west — we must limit our view to the far westernmost group of Slavic peoples west of the Oder and east of the Elbe rivers. It is this group of Slavic tribes, shown on the map which are most often referred to as "Wends." I will use very little in the way of comparative evidence, though detailed studies primarily of other Western Slavic groups, such as the Czechs and Poles, and secondarily of East Slavic and South Slavic lore would reveal many more insights. My own limitations, as the author must also be borne in mind. I am not versed in Slavic philology and am not a specialist in Slavic languages. My chief hope is that this study may in some way inspire another, or others, to carry the work to deeper levels to discover more fascinating information and insights. Such individuals would have to become versed in Slavic studies and do much work in the Wendish regions in what is now the eastern part of Germany.

The Wends have a noble heritage which stretches back further in time than any individuals can trace their ancestry today. These are the deep roots which reach beyond what is called "history" into the souls of the entire folk. This is the shared tradition of all peoples of Wendish heritage— whether in Germany, Australia, or Texas. This little book is about the beginnings of this noble heritage, for from the study of the roots the character of the later branches can be known.

Stephen E. Flowers
Woodharrow
March 2, 1999

Chapter I

Who are the Wends?

Wendish Ethnography and Language

Before delving into the mythology and ancient religion of the Wends, some attention must be paid to defining the tern "Wend." The term is ambiguous because it is one of those names typical in the history of ethnography, which foreigners (in this case Germans) apply to a people irrespective of that people's own self-designation. So the term "Wend" (German *Wenden*, Old English *Winedas*) was one used early on by the Germanic peoples (Germans, English, Scandinavians) to characterize a certain group of Slavic tribes who settled east of the Elbe river after about 600 CE. Germanic tribes who had inhabited the region up to this time were then migrating to the west and south, leaving vast territories virtually uninhabited. It is likely that the ultimate origin of the term "Wend" lies in the tribal name of one of the West Slavic peoples of antiquity, the Veneti (or Venedi), who were identified as early as the first century by the Roman historian Tacitus in his book *Germania*. As time went on the term was specifically used to designate a group of West Slavic tribes living west of the Elbe— the Sorbians and the Main- and Regnitz-Wends. More generally the term is also traditionally applied to the Slavic tribes living west of the Oder River. Among the most important of these tribes were the Obodrites (or Abodrites), Wilzi, and Lusati. The Wends of Texas are more precisely to be identified, at least linguistically, as (Upper) Sorbians. They immigrated from the regions inhabited by the Lusati and Milizi around the Spree river. (See map for the approximate locations of these tribes and their neighbors in the ancient period.)

In pre-Christian times, these Slavic tribes lived in close proximity to a number of Germanic tribes to their west. Generally relations between the Germanic people and the Wends was a good one before the coming of Christianity. Schmaus (1953) points to a generally high level of influence of the Germanic peoples on the westernmost Slavic tribes. This situation would change as the Germans became active agents in the process of Christianizing the Slavs. The Christian God had become so Germanized by the time of the "Wendish crusade" that the Wends referred to him as "the German God." (See Chapter V.)

1

Culture of the Wends

When one wishes to describe a culture — contemporary or ancient — there are a number of factors which must be considered in order to arrive at a complete picture. *Ethnology* must be taken into account– kinship, marriage and reproductive practices resulting in biological reproduction and thus the physical survival of the group. The *ideology*, religion, political values,, etc.– all of the symbolic thoughts peculiar to the people in question is by far the most engaging and fascinating aspect of culture– but it needs physical bodies to be reproduced in the group in order to carry it forward organically. Other factors are *material* culture– which encompasses all the physical *things* (objects) which members of a given culture produce. These objects — the artifacts studied by archaeologists — are often the only windows available to us through which we can view ancient cultures. Finally, we look at *linguistic* data– the language of the people, its vocabulary (which gives even more direct insight into the minds of a people) and structure.

To summarize these factors of culture we might construct a "culture grid":

Culture

Ethnic	Ethical (Ideological)
Material	Linguistic

Then it becomes our task to discover as much as we can about all four of these cultural categories in order to arrive at a more complete picture of a people.

The point of the present study is merely to fill in a portion of the archaic ideology of the Wends– their native religious mythology as it existed before the introduction of Christianity began to blur the indigenous system of spiritual values.

Wendish Cultural Roots

Wendish cultural roots lie in the vast world of the Indo-Europeans. "Indo-European" is a term which identifies a family of languages and cultures stretching from the plains and mountains of the Indian sub-continent all the way throughout Europe.

2

It is most likely that the Indo-European culture spread in a series of waves of sometimes slow and at other times rapid migration, from a much speculated upon *original homeland* somewhere north of, and/or between the Black and Caspian Seas. The date of the onset of these migrations is put variously between 4000 and 2000 BCE. Their culture and language most likely spread in a way very *unlike* the European settlement of North America, for example. Typically the Indo-Europeans probably entered a region as a small conquering minority, made up mainly of male warriors, who then intermarried with females of the indigenous local nobility and in a matter of a few generations the Indo-European culture (language, religion, political structure, etc.) was imposed on the local cultural matrix largely by means of *prestige* rather than physical force. The preexisting local culture is known generically as "Old European." This old culture did not die out entirely, but many elements from it were incorporated into the Indo-Europeanized culture, just as pre-Christian elements would later survive the attempt to Christianize the Wends.

This simplified "family tree" of Indo-European languages shows the position of *Balto-Slavic* — the linguistic group to which the ancient Wends, or Sorbians, belong.

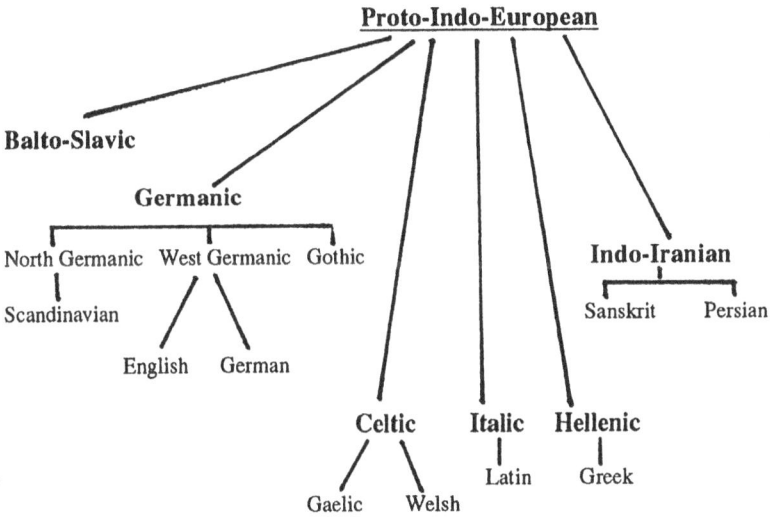

This graphic makes clear that the Slavs are linguistically and culturally linked to peoples who stretch from the Indian subcontinent to Europe, and that their ongoing relations with the Germanic peoples or the Iranian tribes were really contacts with cultures which whom they ultimately share a common heritage. This perhaps helps explain why relations with these groups was so fluid, at least in the pre-Christian times. They shared common cultural basis in religion and world-view as well as language.

3

The Balto-Slavic group is further articulated by several branches of its own family-tree as well:

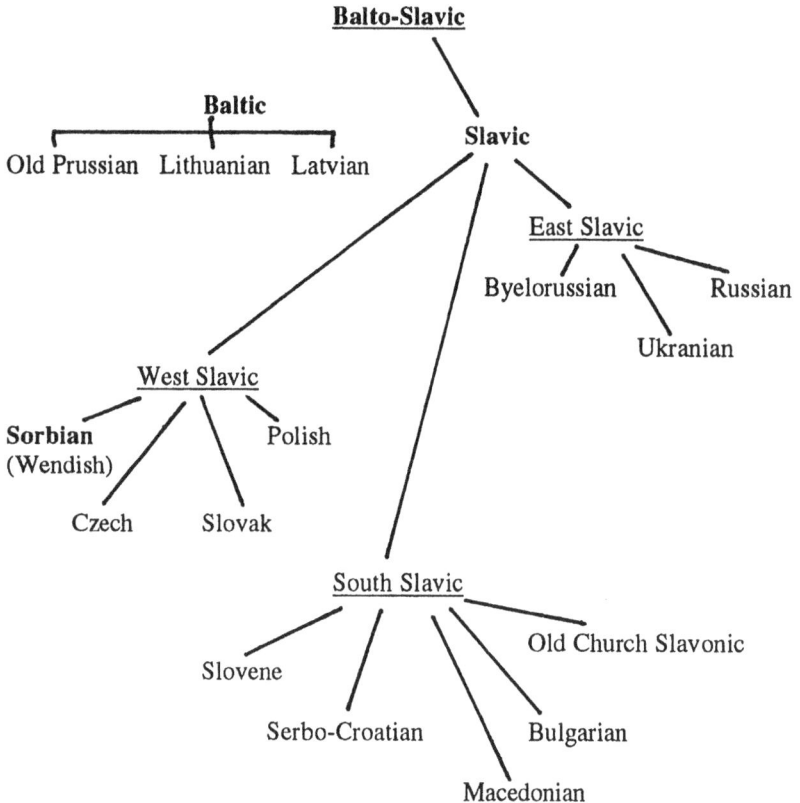

The origin of the Slavic peoples can generally be placed as far back as 2000 BCE in a vast region somewhere around the headwaters of the Vistula and Dnieper rivers. The matter of the exact original homeland of the Slavs is fraught with scholarly controversy. J. P. Mallory concludes: "It is difficult to deny that there existed a geographical center weighted between the Vistula and Dnieper which is most commonly agreed to be Proto-Slavic and which appears to display a continuity of cultural development from about 1500 BCE (or earlier) to the historical appearance of the Slavic peoples."(1989: 81.) From this time to the 5th century CE the Slavs enjoyed a cultural and linguistic unity called the Common Slavic period. During this time the Slavs were exposed to extensive influence from the Goths (a Germanic tribe) and from Iranian tribes called the Scythians and later the Sarmatians. Many words and concepts were borrowed from these cultures during this time.

At the conclusion of the Common Slavic period the Slavic tribes of northeastern Europe began to migrate in an eastward direction, where they displaced the Balts and Finns, and to the Balkan peninsula where they made extensive incursions into the Byzantine Empire.

Historically, the oldest texts in Slavic date from the 9th century CE. These are in what is called Old Church Slavonic, a form of the language developed by the Christian missionaries Cyril and Methodius.

Although there is a high degree of linguistic uniformity among the various Slavic languages, there is no corresponding mythic uniformity. For example among the ancient Germanic peoples: Germans, English, Norse, the linguistic unity is reflected in a mythic unity wherein we find the names of gods and goddesses corresponding. The "high god" of the Germanic peoples was Wuodan to the ancient Germans, Wōden to the Anglo-Saxons, and Óðinn to the ancient Norse. Each of these names is linguistically derived from a common source (*Wōðanaz). Among the Slavs, however, the myths, god-names, etc., diverge widely. The fact that there is a great deal of uniformity among the various languages, however, is suggestive of deeper cultural connections which are simply not reflected in ways as transparent as those of the neighboring Germanic peoples.

Geographically, linguistically and culturally the Wends are especially closely related to the Poles and Czechs (Bohemians). Because later the Sorbs (Wends) were for centuries isolated within a German-speaking majority, their language was at a disadvantage. Today the language is spoken by no more than 60,00 persons mostly in the German federal states of Saxony and Brandenburg in the eastern part of Germany. But even this is a testimony to their cultural tenacity in the face of overwhelming cultural odds.

Chapter II

Traditions of the Household and Nature

Theories concerning the development of Slavic religious mythology have been categorized in three different ways by E. Polomé (1983). 1) Lower level beings, such as the ones discussed below could have been elevated to the status of greater gods and goddesses in the Common Slavic period. 2) Local divinities could have coalesced into a more general pantheon in relatively later times. 3) The religious system may have developed in conjunction with contact with Iranian religious systems. Each of these theories has its weaknesses, and none of them is entirely satisfactory.

As there is no comprehensive ancient source-document for Slavic (or more particularly Sorbian) mythology, much of what we know of how the Slavs expressed their relationship to the sacred world is focused on the simple household beliefs of the people. Some scholars have even argued that there never was a unified great mythology, such as we find of the Greeks or the Germanic peoples, but rather a loose and amorphous set of ideas which emerged from folk practices.

The Soul and Power

In order to begin to understand an ancient, traditional and authentic religious culture, one must understand its concept of the soul and of the world-order in which the soul exists. The ancient Wends possessed a complex and coherent set of ideas about these things which were not dependent on religious doctrines which have to be learned in schools of theology— the ideas were inherent in the language and experience of the people. With the coming of Christianity and the imposition of a *universal* (i.e. not culture-specific) and foreign system of ideas much of the old authenticity was lost. Some of the old concepts are only dimly remembered in folklore.

The soul (Sorb. *duša*) is a repository of *power* for the individual. It is not bound by the physical body, and so it is not bound to the life or death of that body. In ancient times many of these soul-structures were linked to the family and clan— and as long as the life of the clan continues, the soul of the all its members remained immortal.

7

The souls of sleeping, or otherwise unconscious, individuals were thought to separate from the body of the sleeper and fly out of the house and make their ways to the mountain-tops. There they often did battle with the souls of others. To the bodies of the victors in these battles went great benefit and success in life. Some people could lie unconscious for days and their souls were thought to visit the other-world, or heaven or paradise. Those who had seen the otherside could then return, and report on their visions to the people.

Slavic lore has much to report about what have been called shape-shifters— those who could change their physical appearances into animals or even apparently inanimate objects. The best known of this type of person is, of course the werewolf, or Vrkolák. Some such individuals were thought to have become werewolves in an involuntary manner. These were those who had been, for example, born feet first, or with teeth, or those who might have been enchanted in some way by an evil sorcerer. However, more commonly the person became a werewolf *voluntarily* through sorcery. (Máchal 1918: 228-229.)

The whole subject of the werewolf in Slavic tradition should be understood within the context of the ancient Indo-European warrior-cult in which young warriors were thought to be able to transform themselves into wolves in order to fight. Here again this Slavic feature can be compared to an Iranian one where we find stories of the *mairya*, the "two legged wolves," who are in fact young warrior initiates of the man's societies. (Ridley 1976) In the most ancient times the werewolf seems to have been more "super-hero" than "monster."

Another aspect of the powers of the soul somewhat related to the Vrkolák is the *mora*. A person is said to be a *mora* who is possessed by such a spirit or soul. This is a feminine entity which is emitted from the physical body while the possessed individual is asleep. It wanders abroad at night and assumes various shapes as it approaches people's houses and, after causing them to fall into a pleasant slumber, enters their bodies and sends them terrifying dreams. It especially sets upon children and it can choke its victims and even suck their blood.

This obviously sounds much like the famous vampires of Slavic lore. Schneeweis (1953: 75) reports that the belief in vampires was well-known among the Sorbians— as among the other Slavic peoples. Hard evidence for the belief in vampires in the distant past in specifically Sorbian territory is attested by discoveries of skeletons in ancient cemeteries which have knives, nails or pieces of iron piercing down through the lower jaw into the chest.

Ancestor Worship

The ancient Wends, like all their Indo-European cousins, were much involved with ancestor worship. The semi-legendary tribal patriarchs served as patrons of the families and they enjoyed enormous respect as it was expressed in certain religious ceremonies, such as the offering of drink to the gods and the departed heroes.

8

An important religious practice which tells us much about the regard the ancient Wends had for their ancestors is that surrounding the treatment of the bodies of the dead. Before the 9th to 10th centuries, that is, before the influence of Christianity was felt in the land of the Wends, the general method of treating the bodies of the dead was cremation. The ashes were then gathered and buried in urns, or mounds were raised over the site of the funeral pyre. It also often happened that horses and/or young slave girls were sacrificed and burned with individuals of high rank, especially warriors and tribal chieftains. Barley was spread over the ashes or mixed with them, perhaps as a link with the cult of fertility, or as a symbol of the recurrence of the human spirit. This use of the barley grain is very old, and common to the Indo-European heritage, as we find mention of it in Homer's *Odyssey*.

After the 10th or 11th centuries, marked by a growth in Christian influence in the region, there is an increase in the use of inhumation graves. The dead would then be buried with grave goods, such as food and valuables, such as coins, semi-precious stones and ceramic eggs.

Whether we are talking about the sacrifice of horses or the presence of coins in the grave, in all instances the practices reveal the people's firm belief in some sort of a life after death. The dead will need the things being sent with them when they are on the "other side."

Many ritual elements existed which were obviously meant to ease the transition of the dead from this world to the next. This was apparently motivated not only by a love of the dead individual and a desire to ensure that this individual meet with a good after-life, but also by a certain *fear* of the living with respect to the dead. The ancient Wends, like all other ancient Slavic peoples, believed in the possibility of the evil dead rising from their graves to seek the blood of the living. Those who were so feared were likely to be men or women who inspired some kind of fear in their own lifetimes, who were considered outsiders, or perhaps insane. Certain steps were taken to ensure that such corpses would not rise up to molest the living: They were buried in extraordinarily deep graves, large stones were piled on top of their bodies, their bodies might be nailed or staked to the bier, they might be buried face-down, or their heads might be turned around backwards.

One scholar, Unbegaun (1948) maintained that the chthonic, or "underworld" element generally seems to be lacking in the old Slavic religion. Commonly there is a clear distinction between the cult of nature and that of the ancestral spirits. But there is also some conflict between these two expressions of religion. Unbegaun claimed that the chthonic, or darker, aspects of Slavic religion were to be found in a specific aspect of the ancestor cult— that is, the widespread belief in, and fear of, the vampiric dead.

The human head played an important role in the religious conceptions of the ancient Wends. It was thought to be the seat of the human spirit and the initiator of all action. The head was in and of itself a symbol of human individuality and identity— or the individual potency of a god. This is the reason why the head was used so often as a symbol in the construction of temples and one of the reasons why the Slavic gods were depicted with multiple heads.

On the negative side, the heads of enemies were sometimes *hunted* by the ancient Slavs, as they were by the Celts. The heads of the enemy were often placed on the gates of fortresses or temples. It was in front of the temple of Svarožić in Rethra that the head of the Bishop John of Mecklenburg was displayed in 1066, after the successful uprising of the Wends against their conquerors.

In the final analysis the ancient Wends, like all their other Indo-European cousins, maintained a special spiritual relationship to the spirits their own ancestors, whom they worshipped as virtual gods. With the coming of Christianity, this practice would be transferred to the "cult of the saints," but in pre-Christian times the "holy ones" were not just those who were heroes of the church, but rather most especially the heroes of one's own clan and tribe.

Household Religion

The Slavs, like most other traditional peoples, had a well-developed *household* religion. The focus of everyday spiritual life was not so much a "church" or temple— but rather one's own house. Although the official old-religion eventually disappeared, in many Slavic areas aspects of this household religion maintained themselves right into the 20th century, often in the form of what might be called folklore.

Every household was thought of as a sacred space. Various parts of the house had special symbolic meaning. Curiously, in almost all Slavic regions it is found that people believe that the space between the hearth or oven and the wall is especially loaded with power. It is here that many household gods live and from here their influence in every corner of the house can be felt.

We know that this folklore has deep roots. The Chronicler Thietmar reports of the Wends that: "They worship their own domestic gods and hope earnestly for their help and sacrifice to them." The archeological record shows a wide variety of small figurines which are apparently gods and goddesses which the people carried with them in pouches.

That the ancestral household gods, called *penates* in the Latin-language chronicles of the Middle Ages, could be transported with the people as they migrated form land to land is attested in the *Chronica Boëmorum*. The author of that chronicle, Cosmas, reports that Czech, ancestor of the Czechs, carried his *penates* on his shoulder as the Czechs entered Bohemia. When he saw the new land he said to his companions: "Rise good friends and make an offering to your *penates*, for it is their help that has brought you to this new country destined for you by Fate ages ago."

Each home had its ancestral household god. This might be called a *džěd* in Sorbian, which also means grandfather, or it might be called a *pomocliwy kubołćik*, or "helpful kobold." This entity especially liked to live in that special space between the oven and the wall. In Russia this entity is called the *domovoi* (Sorb. *domowy*) and he sometimes has a his wife, called a *domovikha*. There is also a tribal god called a *Rod* or *Chur*. Other lesser divinities populated other parts of a farmstead— the further one moved out away from the house the more unfriendly these entities might become. They would sometimes have to be appeased with offerings of bread and/or beer. Such beings become most dangerous in the forbidding forests surrounding most cultivated land in ancient times.

Household spirits often took the shape of serpents or small dragons. In Sorbian territory this is called the *plon*. This devilish entity had its origins outside the house, but would arrive, flying as a ball of light, down the chimney into the house into which it is called. It will help provide wealth and well-being in the household, until it might be asked to leave.

The Lusatian Wends believe in the *Lutki*, or "little people," who are very similar to the dwarves in Germanic myth and legend. These *Lutki* are sometimes said to have been the original inhabitants of the land. They are seen as having disproportionately large heads and large protruding eyes. They dress in bright colors and wear large hats and red caps. The *Lutki* live in the woods or in the mountains in underground dwellings. They are great craftsmen and taught humans how to build houses. These "little people" are gifted in prophesy and in the musical arts. They fit into the household religion in that they become attached to a single human household and help it in various ways. But they love to fight with the *Lutki* attached to the households of other humans. As usual, they help those who help them and punish those who offend them.

Nature Spirits and the Cult of Nature
From Wild Women to Water-Men

The ancient Slavs appear to have had an especially close spiritual relationship to nature. Not only did their great divinities have links to natural forces — such as the sky, sun, or fire — but also other aspects of nature such as fields, plants and water were populated with entities with which humans could develop special relationships. These relationships are usually beneficial, but because the entities in question are awesome and sometimes frightening, their effects can also sometimes be detrimental to human contacts.

It is widely thought that the ancient Slavs especially worshipped the sun, as well as other heavenly bodies as embodiments of the divine. It was widely believed that these was a special relationship between humans and the stars, as it is said that there are as many humans on earth as there are stars in the sky. Upon birth everyone receives a star, and when death draws

11

near, that star falls from the sky to earth, as the soul of the person rises to heaven. (See Máchal: 1918, 273.)

Among the Lusatians there are many stories concerning the *džiwje žony*, or "wild women." (See Máchal 1918: 263-264.) They are seen as good looking women with large square heads and having long thick red or black hair. They live underground in dwellings similar to those of humans. These wild women know the secret forces of nature and how to prepare plants and herbs for magical purposes. They are fond of music and singing, and often invite young boys and girls to dance with them. Storms are thought to result from their wild dancing. These wild women of the forests often also lure young boys into marriages with them.

Like many other similar beings, they are often friendly to humans who make offerings to them. They repay these offerings with various services, such as keeping the house clean, or helping out with the harvest. They can even help ensure a bountiful harvest for those who honor them. However, if somebody insults them or otherwise misbehaves, they can also be punishing. Sometimes when they have children, one of the *džiwje žony* will leave her child in the place of a human one who is not being properly cared for by its own mother. The *džiwje žony* often reveal themselves daily at noon or at sun-down, but they are most powerful on midsummer night (June 21).

The *připołdnica* is also the subject of many tales among the Lusatian Wends. (See Máchal 1918: 268.) She is seen either as an old woman dressed in a long white gown or as a young girl. She appears at midday in the fields and engages those who she finds working there at that time in conversation. They must be able to talk to her for an hour about one single subject or risk either loosing their heads or becoming very ill. Sometimes she will put questions to them about technical matters surrounding the raising of flax or hemp. The farmer must answer these questions correctly or be punished. This entity is also referred to as the "midday witch" because her effect is almost always harmful and fearful. It was also thought that a new mother would have to guard her child most closely during the hour between twelve noon and one o'clock to keep it safe from the *připołdnica*.(Schneeweis 1953: 7.)

Other entities that populate nature include the *wódny muž*, or "water-man." This entity lives at the bottom of bodies of water, such as lakes or ponds. The effect of contact between humans and the *wódny muž* can be either beneficial or detrimental for the human. This is in contrast to the *błudniki*, or "will-o-the-wisps." These are friendly entities which appear as balls of light in the dark forests and swamps to help humans find their ways back home when lost. This phenomenon has, of course, been connected to the natural phenomenon of swamp gas—phosphorous gas rising from stagnant bodies of water. Another group of strange entities are the *graby*. These are male creatures of small stature but extreme strength. They are so powerful they can tear horses apart— and they often devour horse-flesh. (This later trait would identify the pagan heritage of these entities.) *Graby* even have horse hooves themselves. These they like to stick through windows of rooms where girls are gathered while engaged in spinning or other activities— thus frightening the girls terribly.

In prehistory birds, and especially fowl or poultry, played a large role in religious symbolism. The egg of such birds was the chief symbol of fertility— of the ability of one thing to regenerate itself in a way which borders on the miraculous when one stops to think of it. This led to the practice of the creation of symbolic eggs, which are still produced today in Slavic countries. These "Easter eggs" were often made of glazed earthenware. These were traded widely in the region in ancient times. Examples of such Wendish eggs have been found as far away as Scandinavia, so they were apparently used as valuable trade commodities even then.

A continuation of the importance of birds in the lore of the Wends is found in the customs surrounding the "wedding of the birds" (Sorb. *ptači kwas*) which takes place on 25 January. As a children's custom this takes the form of the children leaving out empty plates at night to find them filled with goodies left by the birds who want to share their good fortune with the children on their "wedding day." Like so many children's celebrations in all cultures, this probably started out as a custom to honor the ancestors, who were in fact thought to be reborn in the children.

As with other traditional peoples it would, in the final analysis, be a mistake to call the ancient Slavs simply "nature worshippers." It only may appear so from a medieval Christian perspective which did not recognize anything sacred or holy *within nature*. It might be said simply that the ancient Wends had a concept of the divine which encompassed *both* nature and a transcendent spirit.

Chapter III

Tradition of the Holy
Temples, Icons and the Priesthood

The Idea of the Holy

Archaic and traditional religions have as an essential part of their practice the regular management and experience of the *holy*. This idea of the holy is something which could be *felt* and experienced by traditional peoples. It is often the case that this holiness is felt in two very different ways. One is something which is perceived as being something *wholly other* from everyday experience. When an individual encounters it a feeling of awe and even terror may overcome that individual. This is what Rudolf Otto termed the *numinosum tremendum*. On the other hand there is the feeling of holiness which makes the individual feel safe, secure and protected from harm– a feeling of being profoundly *at home*. This is what Otto called the *numinosum fascinosum*. In Sorbian the world for "holy" is *swjaty*, forms of which are universal throughout the Slavic dialects. Scholars have determined that this word was one of those borrowed by the Slavs from the Iranian dialects of the Scythians and Sarmatians.

The Wendish temples, and the priesthood who managed them, were institutions designed to deal with the powers of the holy to the mutual benefit of the gods and humans. Among the other aspects of Wendish religion, it is certainly the temples and the priesthood about which we are best informed.

Wendish Temples

In the earliest times the Wends most likely worshipped their gods in outdoor sites and groves, and only later, in the 11th to 12th centuries did they start to build more elaborate structures. This elaboration is thought by some to have come as a result of the influence of the Scandinavians.(Palm [1937]; Schmaus [1953]). Herrmann (1970) notes, however, that the region in question was historically also under Celtic influence from extremely ancient times, and speculates that it is the Celts who may have had a hand in influencing the Wends to build more elaborate temples.

We are best informed about temples in the northern parts of the Wendish territory (that closest to Scandinavia). It is likely that in the more southern regions of the Sorbs and Lusatians the more archaic practice of worship in open-air enclosures and groves was preserved for a longer time. It is also the case that the names of the gods dwelling in these temples are well-known from the north, but virtually unknown from the south. Herrmann (1970: 310) indicates a Sorbian etymology for Schkeitbar east of Lützen. He derives it from Sorbian *swięty-bór*: 'holy grove'. These groves and other enclosures, which may have looked like fenced-in areas bordered by wooden poles and fitted with wooden pole-like sculptures of the gods, would be easily destroyed in later times and would have barely left traces in the archeological record.

However, the great temples — for example those in Arkona, Rethra and Gross Raden — left impressions not only on the physical level, but also in the minds of those who saw or heard reports of them.

The chronicler Thietmar of Merseburg says of the temples: "Every district of this [Wendish] country has its temple and its special idol worshipped by the infidels." The archeological and other records seem to bear out the observation that each district, each tribal area, seemed to have its own temple or place of worship, and that each one seemed to have its own special god-form.

Concerning the temple at Rethra (or Riedegost), and the god called Svarožić housed there, Thietmar says:

> The outside (of the temple's walls) are decorated, as far as one can tell, with different finely carved images of gods and goddesses. On the inside, however, there are gods fashioned by human hands, each with its name carved into it; they are terrifying dressed in their helmets and armor. The highest of them is called Svarožić and all the heathens respect and worship him especially. Also their (battlefield) banners can only be taken away from there by warriors on foot in times of war.

Illustration 4.1 shows a reconstruction of the temple at Gross Raden. This was a fairly simple, yet elegant, complex approximately forty feet long and twenty-four feet wide. The outermost limits of the temple space were surrounded by a low fence, just inside of which were the walls of the temple structure itself. The interior of the temple measured approximately 650 square feet. The exterior walls were made up of evenly spaced planks with gaps between them. At the top of each plank was carved an anthropomorphic head. Whether these heads were supposed to represent gods and goddesses or ancestors remains a matter of speculation.

Certainly the most famous Wendish temple was the one at Arkona on the peninsula of Rügen. Illustration 4.2 shows an outline of the reconstructed

15

interior of the temple, while illustration 4.3 shows an artist's rendition of what the interior might have looked like. The actual site where the structure stood has fallen into the sea due to natural erosion.

It is from the 12th century Danish chronicler Saxo Grammaticus that we learn what we know about the temple at Arkona, and it is from his descriptions that the reconstructions have been made. He describes a building with one common roof over inner and outer walls. The temple only has one door for entry and exit, but has three window-like openings in the other three walls fitted with iron grates. Most conspicuous, however, is an inner sanctuary created by four pillars between each pair of which was draped a red cloth which created an interior space. Inside this sacred space was the great carved image of the god Svantevit described in more detail in the next chapter.

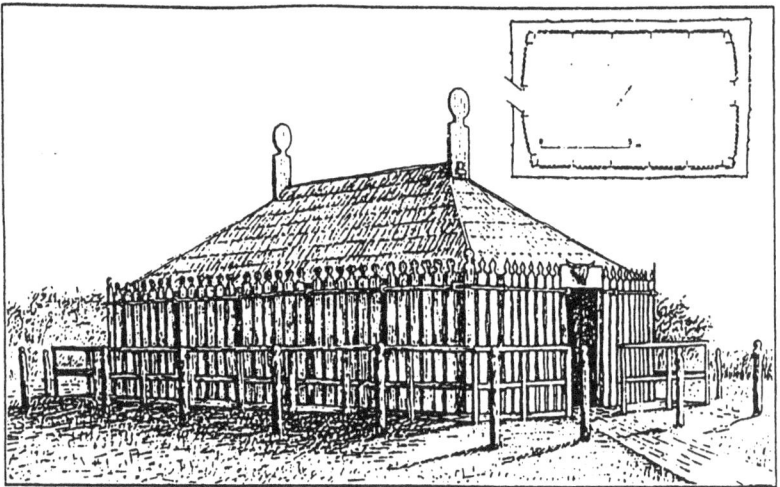

4.1: Temple at Gross Raden

The Priesthood

The temples were the headquarters of the traditional native Wendish priesthood which was by all accounts a powerful and persistent influence in all phases of the people's lives. This priesthood was marked by its activity in what the modern — or even medieval — mind would characterize as political, economic and even military areas. But for the ancient Wends the holy functions managed by the priesthood simply emanated into those areas as a natural expression of the immanent force of the divine. The divinities ruled the world, and so the priests had something to say about how the people— from the peasant to the king — should act in the world.

16

←----------- covered by a -----------→
common roof

←?→

Inner Enclosure

by a cloth

Supported by 4

Standing
Sculpture

posts covered

←?→

↑?↓

The outer enclosure

single
entrance

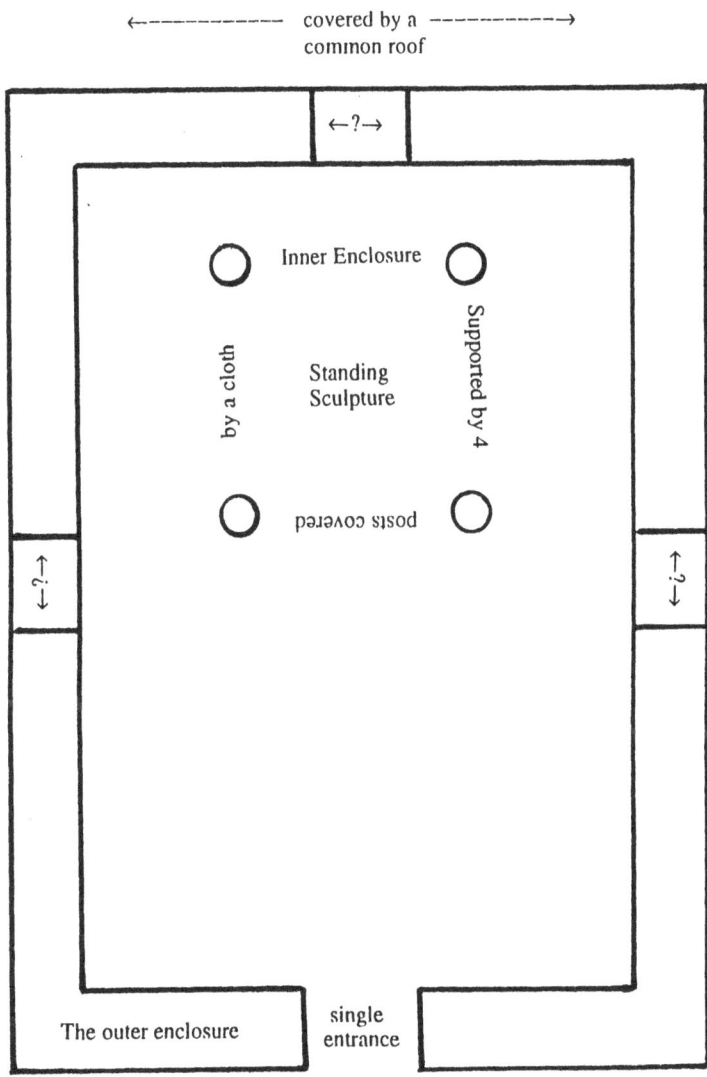

4.2: Reconstructed Interior of the Temple at Arkona

Helmold reports (I:36) that:

> The high priest enjoys a greater respect among [the Wends] than the king. Wherever the lots determine, that is where they send their army. If they are victorious, they put the gold and silver into the treasury of their god and distribute the remainder among themselves.

Wendish priests were skillful politicians, strategists and diplomats. Since they clearly understood the Christianization process as a part of a larger cultural conquest of the Wendish people by foreign interests (e.g. Germans, Danes, Poles, etc.), their political resistance to this conquest was considerable. (See more details in chapter seven of this book.)

The temples themselves were centers of local economic power. For example, priests were largely responsible for granting privileges to foreigners to trade in the Wendish territory. Furthermore, the priests collected a tax to increase the temple treasury– which could then be redistributed in times of famine or other disaster. The priests also cultivated farmland and bred livestock– especially horses. In the legal arena the priests presided over legal assemblies– which met on Tuesdays. (Herrmann 1970: 317-19)

Military policy and strategy was also influenced by the priesthood. The priests had to support all declarations of war for the tribe. Both the uprisings of 983 of the Luitzi and the revolt of 1066 were organized and led from the cult-center of Rethra. Victory celebrations were also held at the temple following the rebellions. It was often the case that priests actually *led* in battle, riding their sacred horses at the forefront of the fight. Or a riderless horse, along with banners from the temple, would lead in battle– and it was thought that the god Svarožić was in command. Similar beliefs were held about horses and the gods Triglev and Svantevit.(Herrmann 1970: 318)

The oracular power of the priests and their sacred horses is one of the best documented aspects of ancient Wendish religious practice. At Arkona there was a herd of horses– and a special holy horse which only the priest could touch or lead to pasture. Using this horse, the priest could decide whether the tribe should go to war. This was done by laying out three rows of spears on the ground in a particular way so that when the priest led the horse out of the sanctuary across the rows of spears, if the horse stepped three times with his left forefoot over the three rows of spears, war was indicated. If, however, the horse stepped over the spears in any other way, war was not indicated.

Such oracles or divination were common to the duties of the priesthood. The priest was thought to be able to transmit the divine will by means of casting lots and the horse oracle. These two methods were often used in combination such that one corroborated the results of the other. If both methods yielded the same result, the given plan was enacted. But if the second method did not confirm the first, the plan was abandoned.

All in all the Wendish priesthood's function was to make and maintain a connection between the people and the land on one side and the gods on the other. At harvest time it is said that the high-priest of Arkona would stand behind a huge honey-cake that was as tall as a man. The priest would then ask the gathered folk if they could still see him. If they answered "yes," he would express the wish that next year they could make a cake so large that he could not be seen. The meaning of this is that he is hoping that the next year's harvest will be even greater than this year's.

4.3: Artist's Conception of the Sacrifice at Arkona

Clearly for the Wendish priesthood the numinous or spiritual aspects of its work were not understood as being separate from what we might be today tempted to call political, economic or military affairs. The ancient Wendish world was one in which the spiritual and material were more integrated and this great *whole* was seen as being something *sacred* which deserved the attention of the ancient priests.

Chapter IV

The Divinities

The Concept of the Divine

The ancient Wends, like the Greeks, Romans and Germanic folk, had many gods and goddesses. The number of them perhaps seems artificially expanded due to the fact that the same god might be known by several special local names. In reality, the traditional polytheist simply recognizes what the religious thinker H. Richard Niebuhr refers to as a variety of *value centers*. These varieties or plurality of centers of value are personified and provided with symbolic attributes which conceal and reveal the character of the divinity within. In fact most "polytheistic theologies" recognize an absolute divinity, but avoid illogically attributing qualities to it (for it is beyond the human capacity to define it)-- and prefer instead to focus on parts of the whole which are temporarily and locally intelligible to the human mind. In many ways, the polytheisms of the ancients were a more direct and honest approach to the divine.

Two suffixed elements are commonly used in the construction of the names of the Gods: -*vit* and -*bog*, Sorbian -*boh*. The element *bog* was borrowed from an Iranian language in prehistoric times. According to Jaan Puhvel (1987) this element comes from and older from **bhāgos* meaning "portion," that is, of riches or goods. Alternately he indicates that it could be used to mean "the apportioner" that is, "god." The concept of the "divine" can be seen as expressed in these two most common ways of saying "god." The word *bog/boh* is ultimately derived from an Indo-European root word: **bhāg-* meaning a "portion" or "share" of something. In the form we have here it is probably meant as a *noun agent*, i.e. "one who apportions (something)." A *bog*, god, is then one who shares out or apportions good fortune or bad, or whatever value or quality of life that god controls. In this a god is seen as an entity which deals out fate, luck, riches and poverty. The suffixed form -*vit* indicates a "bright" or "shining" entity— a characteristic common to many human perceptions of the presence of the divine.

Clearly, then, the two most pronounced aspects of the *divine* to the ancient Wends were 1) the utter *separateness*, or transcendence of being, the god enjoyed, and 2) the beneficial (or detrimental) *interaction* between the god and his worshippers. These two aspects are common characteristics in most theologies, ancient or modern, monotheistic or polytheistic.

One of the most puzzling aspects of the Wendish divine imagery is the presence of *polycephalicism*— that is, they are often depicted with a multiplicity of heads or faces. Some scholars, such as Wienecke, have concluded that this attribute was something invented by Christian monks to make the Slavic faith appear more alien and strange than it might have otherwise. But the majority of scholars agree that the polycephalicism is symbolic of something more profound. First, it might be noted that other mythologies know of such multi-faced gods, the Roman Janus is the most obvious example. This characteristic was also known to the ancient Celts. Herrmann (1970: 311) concludes that "Polycephalicism is apparently supposed to symbolize the responsibility of the god for a variety of realms of activity."

It has sometimes been assumed that the ancient Slavs had a myth concerning the origin of the universe which involved two primeval divinities, one light and one dark. The first was called the "white-god" (*Byelobog*) and the other was called the "black-god" (*Černebog*). The "white-god" was considered to be *above* and the "black-god" to exist in an underworld. It is possible that this mythological pattern is the result of prolonged contact with Iranian tribes (such as the Scythians and Sarmatians) who were the neighbors of the Slavs to the south for many centuries.

But there is also some indication that the Wends had a single god who was all powerful and ruled the others. In his chronicle Helmold reports:

> Among the multiform divine powers to whom they
> ascribe fields, forests, sorrows, and joys they do not
> deny that one god rules over the others in heaven and
> that he, preeminent in might, cares only for things
> celestial; whereas the rest, obeying the duties assigned
> them, have spring from his blood and enjoy distinction
> in proportion to their nearness to that god of gods.

This view is one which is generally in keeping with the organizations of other Indo-European pantheons— with Zeus ruling in Olympus, or Óðinn — also called the All-Father — in Ásgarðr.

Gods and Goddesses
We are lacking in *stories* about the Wendish gods and goddesses— there is nothing comparable to the Norse *Edda* or the works of the Roman poet Ovid. But we know from the historical facts surrounding the early attempts to Christianize the Wends, to force them to turn away from their own gods,

that the people were zealously loyal to their ancient gods and goddesses and often defended their sanctuaries to the death. Such loyalty is not inspired by weak or vague forces. History and time have served to weaken the memories of the old gods— once so strong and vital. The best we can do now is provide a listing of the names of the various old Wendish divinities with their symbolic attributes. At the conclusion of this chapter I will attempt to analyze the common characteristics of the gods in a way which will bring their relationships into better perspective.

On the basis of linguistic evidence or from the standpoint of generalizations from local or regional evidence scholars have speculated widely on the meaning and nature of the old Slavic divinities. This speculative effort has been made necessary by the lack of harder and more explicit evidence.

The various names of the gods and goddesses of the Western Slavs were recorded by men with varying linguistic backgrounds, and often they were completely ignorant of the Slavic languages. For these reasons the forms of the names as they appear in various medieval manuscripts sometimes appear confusing. Sometimes a god's name is recorded only once, and at other times the same god's name appears in several different forms, depending on the spelling system used by the chronicler.

It must also be noted that the names of the gods and goddesses often appear to be descriptive bynames and not the original names of the divinities. This is just like the way in which Jews and Christians might refer to Jehovah (or El, Elohim, etc.) as "The Father," "Almighty," etc. Indeed among practitioners of the traditional religions, as among the Christians, it was often thought to be blasphemous to use the actual name of a god.

Bentis: A god of travelers.

Budjintaja: A goddess of sleeping persons. She protects and awakens them if danger or misfortune threatens.

Dažbog: This is a sun-god, whose name means "the giver of wealth," or simply "the giver." Dažbog is thought to correspond to the god Svarog found elsewhere in the Slavic world. Svarog was also considered a sun-god. In later times the power was typically "demonized" into the midday devil. His name appears to correspond to the Vedic Indian god Bhaga, who was likewise a distributor of divine gifts.

Ischwanbrat: An otherwise unknown divinity of the Sorbs. (= Išvanbrat)

Jarovit: This god is thought to be a Wendish Mars. His name is probably made up of a compound of the familiar -vit suffix and the adjective jaru- "impetuous." His name also appears in a Latinized form as Gerovitus.

Lupa: A Wendish goddess of love.

Plavit: A god of wealth and fortune.

Podaga: He is a god of the hunt, animal husbandry and of the fields. Podaga is also said to be responsible for the protection of fish-catches. This is a god of good weather and gentle west-winds that bring on fertility in the fields. But he is also a god of the storm and of the air. Podaga also sometimes appears in a feminine form as a goddess of Fair-Weather.

Podaga is usually described as wearing a pointed cap, out of which ox-ears can be seen protruding. In his right hand he presses a drinking horn to his chest, and in his left hand he carries a staff. He is the giver of warm days and is called the lover of the goddess of the Dawn— Simzerla. In his role as the lover of Simzerla he is shown as a youth crowned with blue flowers, with blue wings, resting on a bed of flowers.

Porenut: This god was worshipped at Garz on the Rügen peninsula. He is depicted as having five heads, over all of which is a large round hat. He is always shown unarmed. Some want to identify him with Perun, others with Porevit.

Porevit: This is a god of justice, of the earth and of the air. He is generally thought of as a war-god. But he also warns his believers against licentious lust. As such he is a god of marriage, and a protector of the child in the mother's womb. This is also a god of boats and ships. He was worshipped on Rügen together with Porenut and Rugivit. The name of this god is connected with the Old Bulgarian word *pora*, "force, violence."

Porevit is depicted as having five faces, four on his neck and one on his chest. His left hand is held in front of one face in such a way that he is looking through his fingers, while the other hand is on his knee or chin.

Pripegala: This is a god of the Wends living on the Elbe river. In the 12th century resistance by the Wends against their would-be conquerors crusading against them, Christian captives were said to have been sacrificed to him.

Prove: This is a strict and clever god of justice. He is depicted as standing on a column or on a high oaken trunk with a plough share or an iron shield with thirteen bosses in one hand. He sometimes carries a pole with a banner or a sacrificial knife. He wears a crown from which long ears protrude. He is usually shod in boots (and is sometimes otherwise naked). There may be bells on his boots, or he may stand on a small bell with one of his boots. He may have chains around his neck and serpents on his chest.

Oxen and sheep were sacrificed to him, and on such occasions his advice on legal matters was often sought. Sometimes his iron shield was heated until it glowed and a man accused of a crime would be made to touch the shield— if the burns healed in three days, the accused was declared innocent. He may be the same as Prone elsewhere.

Rugivit: This god is generally thought to be a god of the spring-time and of fertility. He is also known as Karevit. This god is depicted in a great oaken statue in a temple at Garz as having seven heads under a single hat. He is armed with eight swords, seven in his belt and one in his hand. Rugivit's image is surrounded by an enclosure made up of red cloths. The swallow is a bird holy to him. Like Podaga, he also has a feminine form, in which he is known as Rago.

24

Simzerla: She is the goddess of the Dawn, and lover of the god Podaga. She is depicted as being clothed entirely in white with a girdle and crown of roses and a necklace of flowers.

Siva: Her name means "gray," or thought by others to indicate "the living one." She is the power of the Earth which brings forth young and nourishes. She is the goddess of luck and happiness. She is depicted as being naked crowned with grape leaves, an apple in her right hand and a bunch of grapes in her left. She was especially worshipped at Ratzeburg. An alternate form of the name, Živa, at times indicated a demonic entity.

Svantevit: His name is derived from *svętŭ,* "holy," and means "the holy-god." It was his image which was central at the sanctuary at Arkona. This giant wooden image had four heads or faces, two in the front and two in the back. Sometimes he is shown bearing an axe and a shield emblazoned with a black ox-head. He can be depicted with a bird on top of his head, wearing armor (or naked), or wearing a long coat carrying a shield and sword. Generally Svantevit is considered the highest god, and a war-god, but also a protector of the fields. His attributes are the bow, a drinking horn, a holy white horse, and a sword.

Svantevit's statue at Arkona held an enormous drinking horn. This was filled with mead at the time of the harvest festival. The condition of the mead remaining in the horn from the previous harvest festival was used by the priests to foretell the next year's harvest.

In Christian times his name was associated with St. Vitus, in whose form he continued to be worshipped by the Wends.

Svarožić: The name of this Wendish god is connected to that of the god known elsewhere in the Slavic world as Svarog. The name Svarožić is a diminutive form of Svarog, which has also led some to identify him as a son of Svarog. He was originally perhaps a god of contracts and sworn bonds among men. He has been identified as a fire god (analogous to the Vedic Indian god Agni). This identification focuses o the function of fire as a force by which elements are bound together toward beneficial purposes. This concept includes processes encompassing everything from cooking food and digestion to the contracts and sworn bonds between and among humans. The concept of peace, *mirŭ,* which indicates a state of mutually binding, sacred, social contract among members of the tribe.

One of his main sanctuaries was at Radigast or Rethra, the stronghold of the Rhetarii tribe of Wends. His image there was an impressive one dressed in armor with a helmet adorned with the wings of a great bird, and a breastplate emblazoned with the a horned black bison— a national emblem of the Wends

Triglav: The name of this god means "three-headed." He is recorded as being present in sanctuaries at Stettin and Wollin in Pomeranian. He has three heads, which shows, according to the ancient priests, that he rules over the three realms of heaven, earth, and the underworld. His faces were covered with golden veils, which indicated that he had no desire to see the misdeeds of humans. (This to some extent is in accordance with the ideas of divinity held by dualists of the Iranian tradition.) Since the name is more a description of his physical form than anything else, it is thought that this was not the actual name of the god. In most respects Triglav appears to be a local form of the god otherwise known as Svantevit.

Triglav continued to be worshipped in the form of St. Ethelbert and St. Peter, as churches built in honor of these saints were built on the hill in Stettin where his sanctuaries once stood.

Zcerneboch: The name of this god means "black-god" or perhaps "black-head"— perhaps better rendered with the spelling Černobog. Such a god is a part of the dualistic religious conceptions which are perhaps an Iranian influence Iranian on the Slavs in ancient times. Helmold mentions this god in his chronicle, where he indicates the Slavs believed that misfortune was dispensed by this "deity of evil." In such a conception it is important to appease and honor this god as well, in order to avoid feeling the effects of his activity.

The Wendish Pantheon

With the over all lack of evidence it is difficult to describe with any certainty the structure of the divine realm of the Wends. It is tempting to make the effort to reconstruct some kind of Olympus (as among the Greeks) or Asgard (as known to the Norse) of these gods and goddesses. This would no doubt be easier if we had more descriptions of the divinities and especially how it was thought they interacted with each other. It is most likely that there was some kind of society or something which approximated a social organization of the gods, as is typical of all the other known Indo-European national religions and mythologies. There is no reason to believe the Wends formed an exception.

The great French philologist and comparativist, Georges Dumézil, by analyzing the myths surrounding the divinities of various Indo-European peoples, arrived at a theory or interpretation of their religions based on a tripartite structure. This threefold interpretation showed how the "social world" of the gods and goddesses of a people was thought to be reflected in the social order of humans in this world.

Dumézil called the various roles which the gods fulfilled "functions"— that is, characteristic actions, carried out by these divinities. The functions are essentially expressions of three distinct kinds of *power*:

1) Sovereign Power
2) Physical Power
3) (Re)-Productive Power

The sovereign power was projected in two complementary ways: through *judgment* and *magical intuition* (communication). In a pantheon we will typically see a division between a god fulfilling the role of a Judge-King and one fulfilling the role of a Priest-Magician. On Olympus this division is between Zeus and Hermes, or in Asgard between Týr and Óðinn. The physical power is projected thought *martial force*. In a pantheon we will find a Warrior-God— such as Ares or Mars in the Classical world, or Thor in Asgard. Warrior-heroes are also to be placed here. The (re-)productive power is variously projected through *fertility* figures or gods of productive arts and crafts. The third group provides wealth, pleasure and well-being. In pantheons we find gods and goddesses of love, beauty, fertility, wealth and craftsmanship. On Olympus we find Aphrodite (married to the smith-god Hephaistos) and in Asgard we have the divine twins: Freyja and Freyr— the Lady and the Lord.

Adam of Bremen describes the temple at Uppsala in Sweden in which three statues depicting the Norse gods Óðinn, Thórr and Freyr are present. These gods represent the three functions: Óðinn the sovereign, Thórr the warrior and Freyr a god of fertility.

Among the Slavs the clearest example of this tripartite system is perhaps to be found within the Russian evidence where we find the triad: Stribog - Perun - Volos. (Littleton 1982: 182-183.) Stribog is described as a "father-god," while Perun is well-known as a "thunder-god" (a trait most usually associated with the second function in the Indo-European system), and Volos is a god of cattle (and hence presumably of wealth).

Regarding the importance of the thunder-god to the ancient Slavs, it should be noted that Procopius of Caesarea mentions that the Slavs worship a supreme deity who wields a thunderbolt and is the recipient of bull sacrifices (*De bello Gothico* III,4).

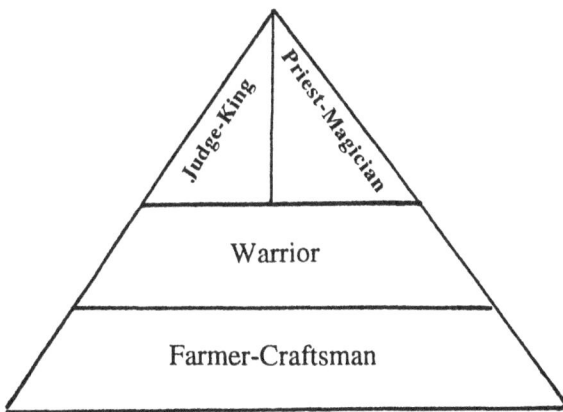

Figure 5.1: Tripartite Arrangement of the Functions of the Gods

Although Dumézil's theories are not entirely accepted by all scholars, they have gone a considerable way toward imbuing the evidence with a deep structural meaning which even speaks to modern-day concerns and situations, be they psychological or socio-economic.

Marija Gimbutas (1987: 356-358) identified three levels of gods in the Indo-European tradition in a way different from that of Dumézil. She saw a system involving a god of "heavenly light" and a god of "death and the underworld" — in other words gods of light and darkness — between which functioned a "thunder god." She also wished to emphasize the "Old European" (i.e. Pre-Indo-European) character of the cult of the various goddesses of the Slavs.

When we turn our attention back to the Wendish evidence specifically, we are at once stuck by the similarities between the divine triad at Uppsala described by Adam of Bremen and the divine triad of Porevit-Porenut-Rugivit reported to have stood in the sanctuary at Garz. Upon review of the scant descriptions of these gods from this and other sources, it is tempting to assign Porevit to the first function, Porenut to the second function and Rugivit to the third. Although other arrangements also seem possible.

Beyond this speculation other gods and goddesses can perhaps be better understood when viewed through the comparative-interpretive lens of Dumézil's theories. It is fairly clear, for example, that the god Prove is of the Judge-King type within the first function, just as Svantevit is of the Priest-Magician type within that same first function field of action. Jarovit, who is even identified by the chroniclers as "Mars," and whose name denotes boldness in battle, would belong to the Warrior-function, while the god Podaga (who also has a feminine aspect) most clearly belongs to the third function. The same can be said of some of the goddesses, such as Siva and Simzerla (who is the Dawn-goddess and lover of Podaga). This aspect of Wendish studies, like so many others, awaits further work by those willing and able to devote a good deal of life-energy to it.

28

Chapter V

The Christianizing of the Wends

Historical Events

The history of the Christianizing of the Wends is a long and often grim one. The earliest attempts to bring the western Slavs into Christendom begin as soon as the reign of Charlemagne (after about 810 CE)— and are not even nominally complete or successful until sometime after the "Wendish Crusade" some 350 years later. Our historical accounts of these times come for the most part from monastic chroniclers who, of course, write from a Christian viewpoint. For the most part the traditional Wends, who for so long resisted not only the imposition of the Christian religion over their own, but also the oppressive feudal state which usually seemed to sponsor and promote the new religion. This history is one of bloody conquest by foreign armies, betrayal by domestic enemies, repeated and often surprisingly successful rebellions and uprisings against the new religious and economic establishment, but ultimately subjugation of the Wends under the banner of Christendom.

From Conquest to Rebellion

From as early as approximately 600 CE the "Wends" — Obodrites, Sorbs, Veneti and Pomeranians — had migrated to areas between the Oder and Elbe rivers, as Germanic tribes migrated to the west and south of these areas leaving sometimes vacant lands and political power vaccua. For 200 years their settlements had become increasingly established in this region. By 805 the powerful Frankish king Karl (Charlemagne) fixed an eastern border of his vast empire called the *limes sorbicus* (the Sorbian boundary). This frontier became established as a result of campaigns carried out by the Franks on the neighboring Slavic tribes such as the Liutici, Sorbs and Czechs between 789 and 812. In one of these battles in 806, the king of the Sorbs, Miliduc, is killed at Werinofeld. The first missionary work began around 810 and was conducted by monks from Regensburg from south of the Wendish territory, and out of Werden from the west.

The usual pattern of Christianization at this time was initial military conquest, then a choice of baptism or death was offered to the leaders of the conquered tribe. One of the most famous examples of when a group chose death over Christianization occurred in 782 at Werden, where over 4,000 Saxon nobles are said to have been put to death for refusing baptism. This initial military conquest would then be followed by political and economic reforms which established a feudal organization of the land with a system of taxation coupled with Christian missionary work conducted from monasteries in nearby regions.

For whatever combination of reasons the process of pacifying and Christianizing of the Wends did not go well. In 858 the Sorbians rose up and killed their installed Frankish conquerors. But the area was at least nominally pacified soon thereafter. Further military campaigns were carried out by the Saxon king Heinrich I in 928-29. These were directed at the Wends living in the Brandenburg region. By 929 the Redari tribe of Wends were ready to revolt— although they were quickly defeated at the battle of Lenzen. In 948 bishoprics were established at Havelberg, Brandenburg and Oldenburg— which should have marked the beginning of the end of traditional Wendish religion in the territory.

But in 955 all hell broke loose as the Obodrites and Wilzi led by the pagan Obodrite king Nakon, along with his brother Stojgnev, rose up in rebellion. Peace was offered by the Saxon king, Otto I, but the offer was rejected by the Wends. They would live free or die. On October 16, 955 they did die in a bloody battle on the Raxa river in northern Mecklenburg.

In the meantime Christianity, already well-established among the Germans to their west, was becoming more consolidated to the north in Denmark and to the south in Bohemia. To the east, the Poles too were being heavily Christianized— although they would also mount sporadic rebellions against the new order.

A generation and a half after the Obodrite revolt of 955, on June 29, 983, a wide coalition of Wendish tribes— Wilzi, Lusatians and Sorbs — led by the Liutizi, rebelled with ferocious intensity. At once the whole Christian-feudal order between the Oder and Elbe rivers collapsed and the missionary work of over a hundred and fifty years was destroyed. It would not be until 991 that the Christian military forces of the Germans and Poles would even attempt a counter-attack. At that time Brandenburg was only temporarily regained. Not until 996 would total control of the region even be nominally regained.

Further to the north, the Obodrites, who had been relatively quiet since their devastating defeat at the Raxa river, once again rebelled with their tribal allies the Liutzi. This, like all uprisings in this struggle was aimed as much at the feudal economic system of authoritarian government and oppressive taxation as it was against the church authority which promoted the economic system. In 1037 the Poles too mounted a short-lived rebellion— but it quickly failed.

By 1043 Gottschalk was able to reestablish the feudal state in the land of the Obodrites— but internal conflicts remained and much of the region was under the control of tribal leaders. In 1066 there was a vast popular uprising against Gottschalk among the Obodrites. Gottschalk was executed and the Wends began to reestablish their native traditions of government and religion. Churches were once again destroyed and the priests driven out.

Around 1100 also Wendish sea-raiders, "Vikings" if you will, began seagoing expeditions attacking sites throughout the western Baltic Sea— along the Danish and Swedish coasts. The sea-raiding tactics used so effectively by the Scandinavian Vikings from about 750 to 1100 were now being employed by the costal Wends.

In 1108 a call went out from the archbishopric at Magdeburg for a Crusade against the pagan Wends. "Crusades" were church-sponsored wars against non-Christian foes: Muslims, heretics and pagans of all nationalities. It would be 1147 before the war-engine could be mustered against the region and the "Wendish Crusade" could begin in earnest. This crusade was designed to destroy the traditional culture of the Wends utterly. In 1150 the temple at Rethra as destroyed. The Danes joined the battle in the north with their king, Valdamar I, and their brilliant military strategist, Bishop Absalon of Roskilde, joined by the German King Heinrich the Lion. This force campaigned from 1160 to 1164. Continued efforts led to the final destruction of the magnificent traditional temple and sanctuary on the peninsula of Rügen in the year 1168 or 1169. This "Wendish Crusade" is what could really be said to be the beginning of the end of Wendish paganism. The religio-political infrastructure of the region, which had been embattled for 350 years, was finally eroded.

It is remarkable when one realizes that it took some fifteen generations of aggressive and relentless military and missionary activity to subdue a region about the size of the American State of Indiana.

The Spiritual Process of "Conversion"

The previous brief chronology of historical events surrounding the Christianization of the Wends only gives the outer appearances of the inner essence of the beginnings of what amounts to a shift in the reality of a people. Such shift in reality, sometimes called *paradigm shifts*, are hallmarks in the history of ideas. All societies and cultures, and even individuals, undergo such shifts though the course of time. These may come as a result of conquest by an outside force (such as we see in the case of the medieval Wends), as a consequence of peaceful contact with a foreign culture (e.g. through trade), or as an outcome of internal development (which might be the innovation of an individual "culture hero" or of a group or organization). In any event the shift is only rarely a quick or simple process.

Such shifts can rarely be *forced*. That is, if the agents of change use brute physical force, those who are the objects of the change — the ones who will ultimately lose power in the process of the shift — will resist and resent it. When the will and determination of the agents of such illegitimate change falter — as it inevitably will — the representatives of the old order will rise up and take measures to revere the trend of change. This is what was happening for the 350 years in which the new order of feudalistic Christianity was being *forced* on the pagan Wends.

It should be noted that the terms "pagan" or "heathen" are not used in a derogatory way here. Both words are derived from Latin and English terms respectively. Both basically mean "country folk." This is because in the early centuries of the development of Christianity the new religion was almost entirely an urban phenomenon. As a city-based movement, people who lived in the culturally more conservative country-side were often thought of as non-Christians.

In the case of the Christianization of the Wends we can identify a fourfold process of development: 1) initial conquest/rebellion, 2) period of mixed faith (Christian/traditional), 3) eventual transition to doctrinal Christianity (Catholic and/or Evangelical), and 4) Romantic yearnings for a return to the *natural religion.*

The first phase is outwardly accounted for in the political and military events between about 810 and 1169. Inwardly these events were made possible by the fact that the new conquering religion had no special prestige among the folk being conquered *and* for whatever reasons the Christian-feudal forces were unable to eliminate those elements within the Wendish tribes which conserved a traditional prestige among the people. Examples of these elements in the society would include the royal blood-lines, political institutions (such as kingship and tribal assemblies of elders) and, of course, the priesthood and the temple sanctuaries they maintained.

The second phase is inevitable in any process of the "conversion" of a whole people to a new way of thinking. The period of mixed faith simply accounts for the fact that not *all* individuals, clans or families are willing or able to "change their minds" overnight. Some *individuals* might be capable of profound personal spiritual transformations in an instant— but even these instances are rare. It is more usual that the new ideas will only slowly and gradually crowd out the old ones over a long period of time and through a number of generations. In some sense the phase of mixed faith is an ongoing state of affairs. Old ideas, indigenous to the folk, will usually persist forever— and those which the Church is unable or unwilling to eradicate will simply be re-institutionalized by the new religion and "allowed" to go on. This is how such heathen practices as Easter eggs and Yule-tide trees eventually became at least partially Christianized.

At some point during this second phase the infrastructure of the old order collapses. This allows the institutions of the new faith to gain prestige in the eyes of the populace without serious competition from representatives of the old way. It is, in the final analysis, only prestige which can cause permanent or deep-level change in a population. People will submit to brute force in order to survive— but they, as a whole, will have no respect for the cultural bullies and will harbor resentment and rebellion in their hearts until the bullies lower their guard. At such times old patterns of culture can be seen to rise up and reestablish themselves overnight as if by miracle. Such things are not hard to understand once one realizes that old traditions are always passed on from parents to children, subtly or overtly, in the secret enclaves of the home.

It is interesting to note that for the most part in the eastern part of Europe the Orthodox Church was much less vigilant in its suppression of pagan elements than was the Roman Catholic Church in the west. In the orthodox world pagan elements were often consciously incorporated into the traditions of the church, whereas in the west this incorporation was done more from the popular side, that is, the people themselves undertook the continuation of the old ways in the form of folklore quite independent of the practices of the church.

Once this "new order" eventually becomes decrepit — often because it was established in a way based on brute force that resulted in a weak foundation — there often rises up a general longing in the population for a spiritual renewal based on national, that is *natural*, traditions. This accounts for an important strain in the general Romantic movement throughout Europe in the late 18th and early 19th centuries— a movement which is strong among the Slavic peoples and which continues today in many forms.

Although in the first part of this book we often had to lament our dearth of information about the substance of the ancient Wendish religion, the magnitude of the resistance put up by the Wendish tribes to defend their way of life bears eloquent and objective testimony to the depth and breadth of that virtually unknown religion. The resistance to foreign ideas imposed by force was fierce and went on for generations. Such a multi-generational struggle could not have been based on vague or confused notions, but rather must have had its roots in a deeply traditional and authentic form of spirituality.

Bibliography

Brankačk, Jan and Frido Mětšk. *Geschichte der Sorben: Von Anfang bis 1789.* Bautzen: Domowina, 1977, vol I.

Callois, Roger. "Les spectres de Midi dans la démonologie slave." *Revue des Études Slaves* 16 (1936), 18-37; 17 (1937), 81-92.

Gimbutas, Marija. "Slavic Religion." In: *The Encyclopedia of Religion*, ed. Mercia Eliade. New York: Macmillan, 1987, vol XIII, pp. 353-361.

Herrmann, Joachim. *Die Slawen in Deutschland: Ein Handbuch.* Berlin: Akadamie Verlag, 1970.

——————. *Frühe Kulturen der Westslawen.* Leipzig: Urania-Verlag, 1971.

Littleton, C. Scott. *New Comparative Mythology.* Berkeley: University of California Press, 1982, 3rd ed.

Máchal, Jan. "Slavic Mythology" In: *The Mythology of All Races* vol III. New York: Marshall Jones, 1918, pp. 217-314.

Mallory, J. P. *In Search of the Indo-Europeans.* New York: Thames and Hudson, 1989.

Nemenyi, Geza von. *Mythologie der Wenden.* (Germanische Reihe, Heft 9) Berlin: Germanische Glaubensgemeinschaft, n.d.

Niebuhr, H. Richard. *Radical Monotheism and Western Culture.* New York: Harper and Row, 1970.

Otto, Rudolf. *The Idea of the Holy.* trans. J. Harvey. Oxford: Oxford University Press, 1923.

Perkowski, Jan Louis. *The Darkling: A Treatise on Slavic Vampirism.* Columbus, OH: Slavica, 1989.

Polomé, Edgar C. "The Slavic Gods and the Indo-European Heritage." In: *Festschrift für Nikola B. Pribić*, ed. Josip Matesić and Edwin Wedel. Neuried: Hieronymous Verlag, 1983, pp. 545-555.

Puhvel, Jaan. *Comparative Mythology.* Baltimore: Johns Hopkins, 1987.

Ridley, Richard A. "Wolf and Werewolf in Baltic and Slavic Tradition." *Journal of Indo-European Studies.* 4: 4 (Winter, 1976), 321-331.

Schmaus, Alois. "Zur altslawischen Religionsgeschichte." *Saeculum* 4 (1953), 206-230,

Schneeweis, Edmund. *Feste und Volksbräuche der Sorben.* Berlin: Akademie, 1953, 2nd ed.

Stone, Gerald. *The Smallest Slavonic Nation: The Sorbs of Lusatia.* London: Athlone Press, 1972.

Tacitus, Cornelius. *Agricola and Germania* Trans. H. Mattingly. Harmondsworth: Penguin, 1970

Unbegaun, B.-O. "La religion des anciens Slaves." *Les Religions de l'ancienne Europe* III Paris: Presses Universitaires de France, 1948, pp. 387-445.

Wienecke, Erwin. *Untersuchungen zur Religion der Westslawen.* Leipzig: Harrassowitz 1940.

Illustration Credits

Illustration 4.1, p. 16 Freilichtsmuseum, Gross Raden
Illustration 4.2, p. 17 After Joachim Herrmann (1970)
Illustration 4.3, p. 19 I. Bilibin

Texas Wendish Heritage Society
Route 2, Box 155
Giddings, Texas 78942

www.ingramcontent.com/pod-product-compliance
Lightning Source LLC
Chambersburg PA
CBHW030030290326
41934CB00005B/570